Belly of the Beast
by Ashe Vernon

WORDS DANCE PUBLISHING
WordsDance.com

Copyright © Ashe Vernon 2014

No part of this book may be used or performed without written consent from the author except for in critical articles & reviews.

1st Edition
ISBN-13: 978-0692300541
ISBN-10: 0692300546

Cover illustration by Kelsey Schreck
Cover design & interior layout by Amanda Oaks
Editing & proofread by Amanda Oaks

Type set in Amatic, Bergamo & Caviar Dreams

Words Dance Publishing
WordsDance.com

*for everyone who has ever felt
too big and too small
all at once*

*this is a book full of ghosts
may you learn to shake them
from your bones*

Belly of the Beast
Ashe Vernon

Kisses That Are All Teeth

Little Red 9
Bad Habits 10
Self Destructive Tendencies 11
First 12
Mercury and Mars 13
Four and Twenty Blackbirds 14
Disillusioned 15
As If In Prayer 16
Deserved 17
House of Athena 18
Speaking of Love 20
Monsoon Season 21
For the Mermaids 23

Blood in the Water

Metropolitan Mermaids 26
This is What Baggage Looks Like 28
Chateau Blanc 29
Decent Exposure 31
Hand in the Honey Pot 32
Small Hands For Moving Mountains 34
Mountains 35
Texas Summer 36
The Gentle Ones 38
Setting Fires 40
Bec and His Boy 41
Son of the Mother 43

A Heart in Flowering Spring

The Mother 46
Two Towns Over 47

Potting Soil 48
Swampland Love Song 49
Venus 50
Best Friends With Benefits 51
I Want To Tell You You Are Beautiful 52
Twenty-Four. 53
But You Leave Them 54
Flashbang 55
Why We Didn't Work Out 56
Sun Sickness 57
Old Souls 58
Delicate Things. 60

About The Author 63

Belly of the Beast

KISSES THAT ARE ALL TEETH

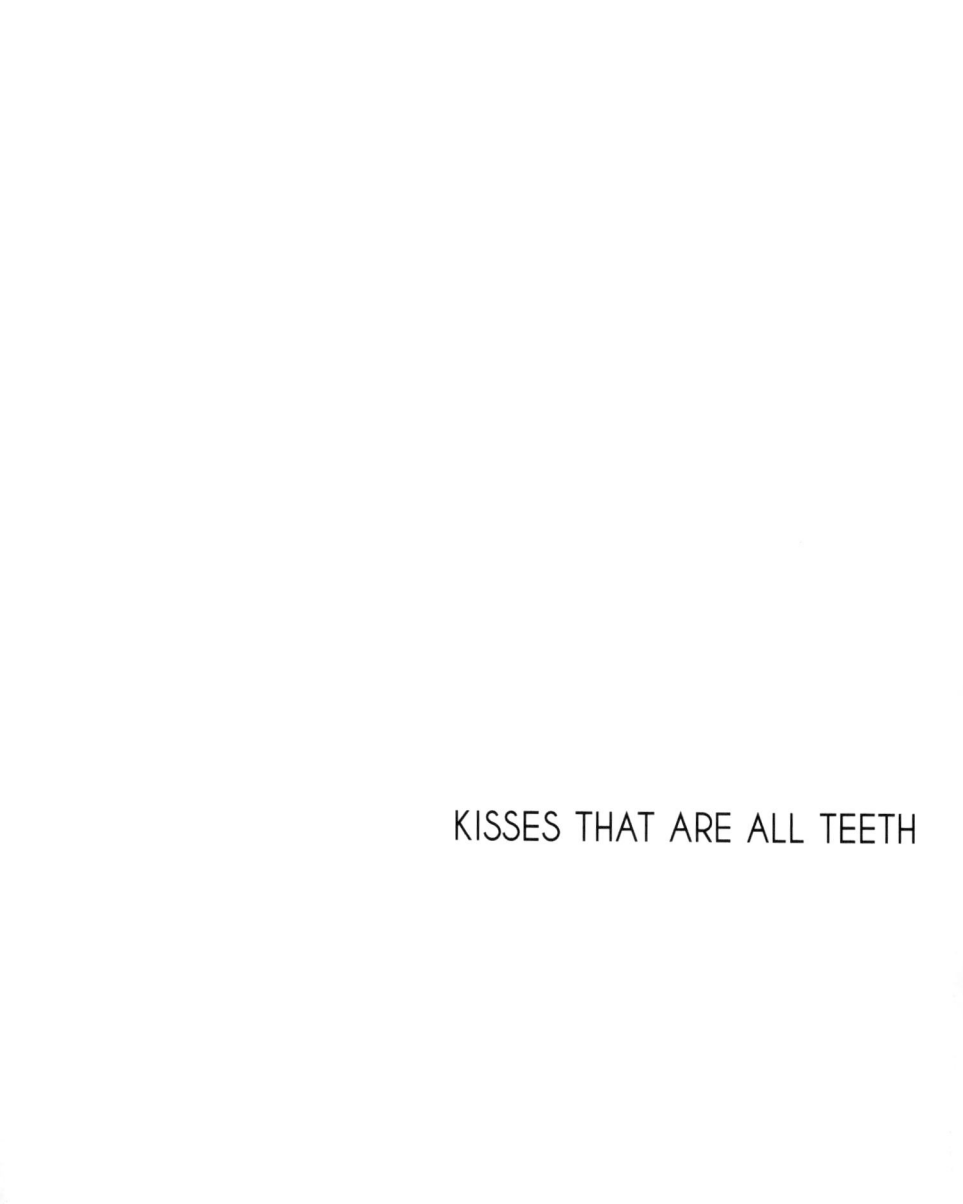

LITTLE RED

I've got a history, made up of
pink-mouthed boys, hollowed out
in all the places I couldn't hold on to.
The cracked scaffolding in my knees
kept winding up to a well-meant "sometimes"
but never quite got there.
I could write myself in circles
talking about the same tongue,
all because I would never be brave enough
to pull it into my mouth—
to finally shut him up—
I'll admit it.
I am a shaking wreck of missed opportunity.
A condemned house that never had a chance.
I went chasing a nowhere
that looked like a somewhere
that I was never going to get.
I rotted from the inside out.
I became the bad part of town:
the woman your mama warned you about.
I was the blood in the water and, oh—
it felt so good
to run so red.
This is the story of how I never stopped running.
This is the story of how,
when the wolves knocked,
I met them at the door
and I became the beast, instead.

BAD HABITS

You were the one who held his hand
after the fist fight that left his knuckles
like red wine on fresh-turned dirt.
All this time, and I always wanted to ask
if his blood on your hands
felt some kind of holy.
I don't think either of us were ever
any good for him.
Because you loved him bruised,
and I loved him bloody—
I know how it sounds, believe me, and
I have torn through rabbit holes
hunting for a better heart,
but I've got a weak spot for broken boys
and that
is my most disgusting feature.
You may not have loved him well,
but at least you loved him halfway whole.
Me? I would have kissed
the broken teeth from his mouth
and kept them all for myself.
I would have cracked open his crème brûlée chest
and eaten out the insides—
hung up his twisted x-rays on my walls
so I could never forget the look of a ruined heart.
I don't break them myself, you see.
I just go collecting in the aftermath.
Grave robber for the still alive:
I may not kill anyone,
but I have never been afraid
to take what I need
to survive.

SELF DESTRUCTIVE TENDENCIES

Religious extremists are
calling this the end,
and you walk to work
with a knife in your back pocket.
And you carry the bones
of the leviathan in your teeth
and you pray to a god
who never saved you,
and your knees
have never been more bloody,
and your hands
have never been more bruised.
And you are lost in a city of wildfires—
one that doesn't love you half as well
as the smoke loves your lungs.
You are spiraling down towards
something you don't know the name of.
And whatever it is,
it's not bravery.
It's setting the sky on fire
and calling it the sun.
This is how you burn out wicked—
not in a brilliant blaze of glory
but like a hearth fire
smoldering out.
It's the goodbye
you didn't think you'd get.
No death of heroes,
just the cold
creeping hand
of your own self-doubt.

FIRST

I didn't love him.
I barely liked him.
But he was heat at the peak of summer,
and he kissed like I was his last meal,
and I was looking for a body to drown in.
Back then, I had a candy-coated heart,
like poppies in the pages of a hymnal,
and he had the thick, calloused hands
of a working man.
He talked like a friend
but he touched like an animal,
and my bubblegum chest wanted that
in ways it couldn't understand yet.
He asked what colors I kissed in
and the poet in me cracked open and spilled over—
exposed like an open wound.
Like all the soft, pink parts of me
I didn't know yet.
He was a means to an end:
my Machiavellian loss of innocence.
I don't regret him,
but sometimes I wish I did.

MERCURY AND MARS

This is how we loved.
Not with mouths,
but with minefields.
We were two bodies starving—
digging through dirt
on the raw of our hands.
I never touched you like
waltzes in moonlight;
I touched like rabid dogs;
like forks in electrical sockets
and I'm sorry for that.
And you: a forgotten era.
You, who crawled
on your belly toward the light.
You, who ate the sun
to keep yourself shining.
You were afraid of the dark
and I was afraid of the dark
inside myself.
I sucked the light from
between your teeth
and left you a dying star
in an unnamed constellation.
I walked up the axis of the earth—
mud beneath my nails,
blood on my chin.
I met the moon halfway
and told her all about
the way I used to feel
when you would kiss me.
She's still the only one who knows.
I took your light,
I'm sorry.
I didn't know I had one of my own.

FOUR AND TWENTY BLACKBIRDS

You and I became a feast fit for kings.
Ravenous for each other,
we devoured our own selves—
rotten peaches on the breath
of the Colossus, no room left
for retribution,
for forgiving one another,
much less ourselves.
We stood our sins up
in a row, nicknaming each sickness
that led us into each other's arms.
We made a game of it.
You would hang promises from your teeth,
pretty as life from the noose,
and I would paint my lips
the color of a bruise
in the hopes it would drive you to want me
the same way my crooked soul
wanted you.
We were a four course meal,
and I dipped my knuckles
through the thick of you,
licked your soft meats from my hands.
I swallowed you whole, but
you always came back.
Your voice an echo in the hollow
of my stomach, your feet digging
into the back of my throat
when you climb from my mouth,
still breathing.
Our little feast of kings.
And for all I thought I wore the crown,
still you laid me on the table,
put the apple in my mouth,
took the knife to the soft of my temple,
and oh so sweetly,
broke me down.

DISILLUSIONED

The boy in the oversized crown
stands with the world on his back
like a coat two sizes too small.
This is the moment you realize you've never
woken up next to someone you were actually
in love with.
That your patron saint is a boy
with tissue paper hands
and wrought-iron ribs
for holding birds in.
The cupid's bow of your lips
was always meant for harp chords,
wasn't it?
They taught you to sling arrows
instead of songs, and you thought them wise.
And him? He makes promises.
Beautiful things, tucked away behind his teeth
like they're waiting for you to find them.
I know nothing of the Ides of March
but I know a sinking ship
better than I know my own heart—
this boy will break.
And when the water pours in,
it will kiss him like his mother never did
and it will be years before the tide
brings him back to the shore.
It's okay to love a drowning man,
but you cannot step into the water beside him.
Remember, you were born with feet,
not with fins.
And treading water can go on for years
but it has to end.

AS IF IN PRAYER

Sometimes I write about you
in the kind of filthy vernacular
a mother hopes her daughter
never learns.
So maybe it isn't love,
but maybe it's something—
sweet in the middle,
rough around the edges.
The kind where we kiss right before
we sink our teeth in.
After all, I am no sacred relic,
no uncovered altar:
I am not a place for pious hands.
Baby, I'm looking for a train wreck
—unkempt, unclean, unholy—
and I keep looking for ways
to make that seem profound.
But the truth is,
I've got no room for poetry.
Not when my hangnail chest
goes hungry
at the mention of your name.
Not when the salt in the wound
is as much exodus as revelation—
now if you would just fuck me
the way you look at me
I might actually have something
to believe in.

DESERVED

Questions keep you up at night.
There are ghosts in the woodwork
and they all look like your mother.
There is someone else behind your teeth
and she beats against your brittle bones
until you shake and rattle like an old house.
You drink in the dust of this place
until it feels like a part of you,
and you pretend like you are not
a patchwork quilt of all the places
that never loved you.
You've woven old heartaches
into the hems of all your favorite clothes;
hung up your histories on the walls;
packed away your mother's smile
in a shoebox in your closet.
There are things you think you don't deserve
and she will always be one of them.
The girl you keep trapped in your chest
is screaming gospel up your throat—
she calls you rare and real and holy.
She wants to love you.
She wants you to know.
But you've gotten so good
at shaking apart
that being whole scares you;
that being loved is the dark horse;
that being loved is the wildcard
worse than the devil you know.
So you don't.

HOUSE OF ATHENA

I met the Medusa on the road.
Hair done up in braids,
she didn't look like much of a monster.
She looked like a woman
who needed a place to call home.
I found her hitchhiking up the Midwest,
with a bottle of malt whiskey
and the clothes on her back.
And together, we chain smoked half of Indiana,
left Wisconsin for dead,
drove up the centerfold of the states
like there was no place left, behind us.
We fucked in the kinds of motels
they don't give names to.
She never turned me to stone,
but she kissed like she saw Perseus in me;
like the snap of her teeth was enough
to cast the demigod out.
See, I knew the stories.
What I didn't know was the truth.
That the creature with the head of snakes
was no more sinister than a frightened girl:
betrayed by the god she prayed to,
cast down for crimes committed against her,
while Poseidon preened in his palace.
Assault in Athena's house—
The goddess gave her venom.
And it wasn't punishment,
it was protection,
so that man could never hurt her again.
I met the Medusa on the road
and what I found
was a woman
with heartache engraved into her skin,
fury seared to her bones.
And we set out towards the dark,
where men aren't mighty,
where the sun can't touch us.

Gorgons of the highway,
scattering statues on the side of the road.
I don't have to be a monster,
to know all the ways,
to turn boys
into stone.

SPEAKING OF LOVE

There is an ocean between
the first time I said "I love you"
and the last time I meant it.
I left that word buried
in the sand of a shoreline I've never seen
and took some time for myself:
to turn my life into a book
that didn't read like unfinished emails
and grocery lists of all your favorite foods.
I spent days scrubbing your name
out of the grout that lines the bathtub,
shaking your dust from my shoes,
relearning how to spell my name.
It must have been
months
of waking up on your side of the bed,
and wondering where all this empty space came from.
I hope my teeth
came tumbling out of your suitcase
the first time you said my name
to a friend in passing.
I hope I hung on like a remora
until kissing her felt too much like
sleepwalking down the stairs of our old apartment.
I hope bad dreams sent you out
to the beach
with a shovel and a good bottle of wine,
digging through saltwater for proof
I ever even touched you.
While you go looking for that word,
I will be at home
in an apartment that looks nothing like you,
drinking hot tea that tastes more like love
than your mouth ever did.
And when you call at four in the morning,
hands as empty as the bottle by your side,
I will be sleeping soundly,
for the first time
in a long time.

MONSOON SEASON

This week,
you've got a heart like the hills
when a storm rolls in.
Even though last week,
it was different:
desert grass beneath
a white and unforgiving sun.
And you know it's bad.
Because when pain like that
turns to an ache like howling wind,
that's when you know it's unpacked its bags
and settled in.
And you—you were so in love.
You thought she'd changed you.
You thought she'd found a heavy soul
strapped to your shoulders
and lifted it free—
that she'd unlaced you a heartbeat at a time
until you could breathe again.
You felt so light in her hands that she
had to be made of something stronger.
She had to.
And you poured all of yourself at her feet.
You thought you were supposed to.
The frightening thing about men
with nothing to believe in,
is that when they find something,
their hearts snap shut like bear traps.
They take no heed of broken bones.
And when she buckled
it's not that you didn't forgive her—
it's that you didn't even know.
Didn't your mother ever tell you
not to love like that?
Didn't she teach you not to take shelter
in other people's bones?
Count to ten.
Lay your hands flat on the table.

You don't have to live and love like this:
all hands—all teeth—no skin.
You are more than a forest fire
trapped in a pair of lungs.
And she deserved better than that
all consuming love;
she deserved better than loving
down the barrel of a smoking
loaded gun.

FOR THE MERMAIDS

I've spent the last few months
trying to figure out
if I was the one
who dragged you under,
or if I was the one
who drowned.

BLOOD IN THE WATER

METROPOLITAN MERMAIDS

You have dreams, some nights,
where great sea monsters,
with salt slick skin
and teeth like the masts of ships,
come hulking from the water
in silent, slippery schools.
Their eyes, colder than their blood, they
wrap their scaled and suckered claws around your wrists
and sing the kind of siren songs
that leave sailors lost at sea.
The beasts in your dreams are soft
like the silken backs of man-o-war:
they grip your arms and drag you under.
You are afraid to breathe—
but you do not drown.
Tentacled, toothy terrors
push mollusks into your trembling hands
and sing you the kind of love songs
only the ocean ever hears.
You awake a gilled and gutted thing:
beached and lonely,
you wake looking for the kind of love
you knew beneath the water.
You fear you will not find it, here.
You have the ocean in your lungs.
You have the voice to drag men under.

THIS IS WHAT BAGGAGE LOOKS LIKE

I've got your name stuck to the back of my teeth
and I taste it in everyone's kisses.
I go looking for love notes you're never going to give me.
Truth is, I fell backwards into your ice water romance,
and the last couple months have barely thawed my fingers out.

I like pretending I've washed my hands of you.
I say your name twenty times a day
and brag about how it doesn't hurt me.
But if you called, I would crash my car
just to say it where you could hear me.

Truth is, I've got a lungful of apologies
that are all supposed to be yours to give.
I tell everyone I know to be brave
and stay away from the ones who hurt them,
but I am selfish and weak and insecure,
and I would take you back in an instant.

CHATEAU BLANC

Sunday night, Mama comes home late
and locks herself in the bathroom.
You spend the next hour trying
to push your heart through the gap
underneath the door, but
she never answers.

The next morning, you get up early
to scrub the blood stains your heart left
in the carpet and can't help but wonder
if she kisses cigarettes the same way
she used to kiss your father.
When you find her in the kitchen
with a knife between her teeth,
you don't ask questions.
You've learned it's better that way.

You don't know much about your mother
but you know she keeps her grandmother's ghost
in the kitchen with all the good china.
You've been grown a long time, now,
but you think that, sometimes, she still
sees you pigtailed and knock-kneed,
pulling at her shirtsleeves.
And you remember being put patiently to bed
with a glass of water you didn't ask for.
And even now, you remember the look
of midnight in your mother's eyes,
and how they never looked the same
by morning.

You don't know much, because Mama
didn't want you to know how it felt
to grow up in a home where you don't look
under the bed for monsters, because
they're asleep in the bedroom next door.
Your mama, she never said.
She didn't want to hurt you.

You don't know much,
but your father buys wine and she pours half
down the sink, when she thinks he isn't looking.
And when you ask, he shakes his head--
"It's just her way, honey.
It's what she's gotta do."

You're older when you finally feel big enough
to confront her about it.
Thirteen rickety years old, when you tell her
he's a gentle man, and that
you've never even seen him drunk.
She wears a look like porcelain
against a hardwood floor
and wraps her skinny arms around you
(when did your mama get so small?)
"You don't want to, baby, you don't want to.
Men on the bottle aren't like men, at all."

You turn eighteen
and she leaves for the funeral of a man
she never spoke of.
And you learn that not all fathers are like yours.
And you start to understand that broken homes
don't always have broken windows.
That cracked foundations can run too deep,
that the wood rots in the walls,
that sometimes the ghosts pour in
and you never see them coming.
You never see it coming
at all.

DECENT EXPOSURE

All this naked sky
and you,
with your shaking hands,
too afraid to take your coat off.

The array of stars gone shy
and bashful
under the gaze of seven billion
watchful eyes.

You undress facing the window.

You think
the moon understands
what it means to feel
exposed; you think
the moon never turns her back
for a reason.

You think the moon
would kiss you like a southern solstice—
peel herself from the sky
and love you for every hour
that the sun's up.

The array of stars
watch the outline of your naked
body through the glass.
They don't love you the way
daytime TV says you're supposed
to want to be loved.

All this naked sky, and
you—
with your shaking ribs,
you—
with your aching hands,
you—
too afraid to love the sunlight.

HAND IN THE HONEY POT

There's a woman in my building
who hides her heart between her legs
hoping that maybe then she might actually
feel something.
See, around here, girls grow up
on the sidelines of their own bodies:
taught their "virtue" belongs to boys
before it ever belongs to themselves.
There are words you just don't say in public
and all of them are slang words for vaginas.

There's a little girl down the street
too young for this kind of heartache.
She sprays perfume on the unseen monster
between her thighs
as a gift for the boy she thinks
she's fallen in love with—
afraid he'll leave without reason to stay,
afraid he'll be too disgusted by
the new hair below her belly
to even touch her.

We grow up grooming the good
from our bodies. Grow up the enemy.
Eve and the apple,
Pandora and the box:
taught women are the root of all evil,
our bodies the fiendish unholy,
temptation incarnate.
Like succubi of the subway—
they call it our own fault
that men become animals around us.

Generations of girls huddled beneath the sheets,
guilty hands between their guilty thighs,
convinced that touching themselves
is the worst kind of crime.
Meanwhile the boys on the street

gather in groups and crow at the breasts
of the girls who pass by.

But boys will be boys, right?
Best to let sleeping bitches lie.

SMALL HANDS FOR MOVING MOUNTAINS

To the daughter I may never have:
I will not raise you to accept this.
I will never let you look at violence
like the hole in the sinking ship you cannot save.
I will kiss reverence into the cup of your palms,
and when you hold them to your rosy face,
they will remind you of all the worlds you can move
with steady hands
and small fingers.

I will teach you the kind of survival
that brings the ocean to the shore.
You may not always love yourself,
but you will know, without a doubt,
that you are worth loving.
And when the monsters come
and try to love you with fists
and heavy mouths,
you will know that love is nothing so
sharp and viscous,
and you will cast them out.

I cannot stop the world crowing at you
but I can teach you how to roar back
with the kind of force
that shakes the birds from the branches.
I cannot make the world soft for you
but I will put a burning in your blood
and enough strength that you will never accept it.
No girl of mine will let herself be told
that she belongs to anything
other than the four walls that she calls home.

MOUNTAINS

For years of my life,
I treated my body like a fixer-upper
or a home improvement project.
Maybe a new coat of paint will
make me worth something this time.
Maybe if we knock out a few walls
and build a walk-in closet,
there will be room in me for all the love
my heart pumps out like blood.
Like tap water.
Maybe I can build a levee to hold it all in.
It took until I was nineteen,
with a Black&Decker buffer,
trying to smooth the cellulite out of my thighs.
It took until I had broken my own back over my knee.
It took until I was aching
from all the empty rooms in my renovated house
to realize that a body is not a rental.
A body is not a work-in-progress.
A body is not something to be ashamed of.
They gave me names that stuck
like coffin nails in my bones.
I gave them years of believing they were right.
I am not a town home.
I am a temple.
Frightened hearts leave their hymnals at my feet.
I spread my arms and take up space, I am sprawling:
eight stories high with a heart like climbing ivy.
They told you lies.
Girls are not just small things
with tiny hands and bleeding hearts.
Girls are big as the ocean with mouths like the Barrier Reef.
Girls carry love in the bend of their shoulders
that could bring a country to its knees.
When I say I am bigger
than the things that try to hurt me,
I mean it literally.
I am not ashamed to be a big woman.
I've had mountains in me from the day I was born,
and shame on you, if you are too small
to reach them.

TEXAS SUMMER

Here, the heat pours sticky and thick—
dripping honey summer Sunday,
like hands, like tongues, like lips.
Here, the sun drags low across the ground.
Here, she walks the roads, heat coming off her back,
and sweats like the boys in the wheat fields,
with the scuffed shoes and the holes in their hats.
Here, the sun works the land—
crawls up from the gulf to sink her fists into the soil:
a sun with dirt on her hands.
She comes through town at high noon,
clouds draped round her hips like peasant's dress:
no high born, wealthy man's sun.
She's a body with labor in her knuckles,
age in the time-worn bent of her back.
She drinks with men from the city,
waits till the moon is full, and wades
waist deep, through the river, just to hear
the steam hiss off her bones.
Here, there's a sun livin' in sin, right off the highway.
She lifts her skirts and baptizes the whole Southwest.
Kisses like she's keepin' secrets,
kisses like she knows best.
See, the sun round here, she never speaks,
but she knows how use her tongue
to make a learned man scream.
Heavy hands like a woman with a history,
like a woman with a train to catch.
You move down from the mountains and
she peels you out of your cotton and tweed,
your businessman clothes.
She licks a love of the land between your teeth,
lays you in the grass of a long forgotten country,
stages wars and revolutions in the space between your knees.
Our sun, she's got stories of bloodshed and conquest—
of white men learning how to take,
of gospel that reads more like slander.

She's no sweet tea, soft lipped, Southern Girl.
You live under her, you take our history with you.
She feeds it to your lungs until it's all you can remember.
Our sun carries the bodies of the broken on her shoulders—
bears her teeth till rednecked men grow weary with the heat.
Here, the air hangs thick and sticky—
dripping honey summer Sunday.
Like hands, like tongues, like teeth.
Here, the sun is starving always hungry.
Here, she drags her fingers through the peat.

THE GENTLE ONES

What they don't tell you
about the gentle ones,
is how we keep all our hurts in cages,
and line them up like circus attractions
on the inside of our own chests.
We carry the weight of them,
and call it surviving.

What they don't tell you
about the ones who grew up
walking tightropes,
is that we only look so graceful
because we never learned
how to climb down
and we call this
remarkable.

What they don't tell you
about the illusion
is that I am as much lion
as I am lion tamer.
And I got good at inflicting pain
the same way I got good
at soothing it.
This, we call unfortunate,
but inevitable.

What they don't tell you
about the gentle ones
is how raw we all are,
just below the surface:
how the roar of the crowd
feels like a city burning;
how we love like immolation;
how we leave nothing but dust
in our wake.

We call this

poetic justice.
What they didn't tell you
about us
is that we've learned so well
that we only have to be cruel
once.

SETTING FIRES

I once saw a girl
with hands like cities burning.
She knelt down by the sea
looking for salt water to put the fires out,
but when the wind kissed her face
she went quiet—
like a lost child.
It was love, written in the curve
of her shoulders.
It was love woven into
her butterbrickle spine.
It was love that kept this girl standing.
Sometimes, the kids setting the fires
are the ones least likely to want
to watch them burn.
See,
some of us are hot coals,
lit up from the inside,
and some of us love so hard
we don't remember how to make it stop.
I saw a girl with hands like cities burning
and I held out arms still singed
from loving where I was not allowed
and we hugged like wood smoke
and I finally forgave
myself.

BEC AND HIS BOY

This is the story of two boys in love.
Boys who never knew any kind of life but running.
Boys who kissed across the train track that carved
through what it was they wanted and what
they were told they could never have.
These boys put their toes to the rails
like runners at the starting line.
No time for that scuffed shoes, knock-kneed,
slow burn kind of love.
They had to love fast
or the train would catch them.
Had to love fast 'cause
they're no use to anyone
dead.

It's the story of a boy named Rebecca—
a boy whose skin was drawn up in the wrong size.
A boy who spent the winter bringing snowflakes to his mama
because he liked the way they gleamed in the light.
It's the story of a boy who hated wearing dresses,
a boy terrified of the nothing between his thighs.
This boy ran before he could walk
and dreamed of the men on Mount Olympus, because
they were allowed to be both beautiful and strong.
This boy, he swallowed his own heartbeat:
grew up in a house where everything
he knew about himself had to be wrong.
And he fell in love with a shipwrecked clutter of a heart
pulled up from the mud, and that bad memory,
bent beak, black eye of a boy,
he had it for him bad,
but he fell in love so good.

His is the story of a boy with a home like quicksand.
A boy with a papa who loved him well
but a papa who loved him bad.
Broken home, broken heart boy
went looking for love in all the hands
he knew could hurt him, because he thought

that's what love actually meant.
They say we all go chasing the ghosts of our fathers,
and this boy, he chased with the worst of the best.
Hard knocks, hard head, hard liquor boy.
He fell in the love with an angel
the next street over:
the one everyone called a girl, but he
knew better, he
loved that boy all the way down
to the parts nobody else knew how to love right.
He loved that brittle boned, round faced, beauty of a boy—
he loved him right.

And they were always one flash flood from falling over,
a city on its way into the sea,
beaten up by the storm off the coastline—a hurricane
through the thresholds of their interwoven fingers,
love in the sea-sick belly of the beast.
They were clasped hands and timid hearts and skinned knees.
Life isn't kind to two boys caught up in dreaming,
it doesn't kiss like lovers at the starting line,
but for all their bruised heart, broken arm, split lipped kind of hoping,
they held each other like the eye of the storm
passing over the rockiest part of the beach.
This is the story of two boys in love,
who set off for the far corners of the sunset,
and ran the rails with the sound of the train at their backs.
They've never loved like people who could afford to take chances.
They love like outlaws on the run,
like comets out of orbit,
like the lit cherry on the end of a cigarette.
They love like they have to.
Like they've got nothing left.
And for them, that's enough. For them—
that's the best they've ever had.

SON OF THE MOTHER

When the god of the forest finally fell,
every soul in the brushland
came out to see it—
the hulking body folding itself
back into the soil,
ivory tusks turned toward the sun.
Best loved by the Earth,
she took him in her arms,
and lifted him up.
The Sky bent down to meet him,
his floral bones in full bloom,
and kissed him with her cloudy mouth.
All together, the Stars gather him
from the Mother's hands—
his bulk like hollow bird bone,
he is weightless in the crook
of the elbow
of the cosmos.
Weightless when the sticky summer air
passes him to the Moon
for safe keeping.
He is the end of an era.
He is the last echo
of a half-forgotten religion:
the Son before there was a Son,
the Hands of God when God
was still the whisper of a bedtime story.
And here, the star-sparked spirits of the soil
bear down in grief.
Here, his planet mourns him.
Here lies the fallen god of the forest:
his, the lungs that breathed your body into being—
his, the altar that never forgot you—
his,
the ivory tusks
that carved you
from the loam.

A HEART IN FLOWERING SPRING

THE MOTHER

The only thing I know for sure
is the Earth pulled us up from the breath of her lungs
with hands the color of mud after a good, long rain.

Between kisses, you tell me the Earth has abandoned us:
ripped us out by the roots, like weeds, and left us for the birds.
You call it inevitable. You call it deserved.

Like the soothsayers of Rome, you talk of a time
when the sea will rise up against us like a soft-feathered army
and we will be lost in the foam.

You claim ribs that rise like an industrial skyline,
but in the dark, I still feel the moss beneath your skin—
your flowering heart, the way you follow the sun like gospel.

Sometimes, I see your mother in you so strong,
I go looking for the smell of lemongrass in the bend of your wrists
and wonder if you'll hold open your door, too, when I go looking for
a home.

Against your neck, I echo whispers of the hum beneath our shoes,
where the ground tells love stories in his mother tongue:
the Earth did not forsake us then, the Earth does not forsake us, now.

We are writing a history in hand prints on the skin of the body
that kissed us alive; she sees our cities and our skylines
and lifts her soil to raise them up.

The only thing I know for sure, is the Earth forgives our unkindness:
that beside your doctrine of revolution, she is a patient mother—
one who loves her children.

Even when they forget how best to love her.

TWO TOWNS OVER

I've got a heart that always lands a few cities over.
I'm trying to make a home and she
is navigating the highways back to me.
I don't define myself by love,
but by the absence of it,
like negative space in a painting:
these are the years I pulled myself up by the roots
and those are the ones where I dug through my ribcage,
into the meat of my lungs,
looking for dinosaur bones.
I write my heart letters, sometimes—
long distance phone calls to the muscle in my chest
just to see if they're treating her right.
I ask her if the stars where she is look more friendly
than the unwashed dishes in my kitchen sink;
I tell her how they've started to look
like a toothy skyline beneath the faucet moon.
I've spent years feeling like
the right person under the wrong sky,
and maybe my meandering heart has got it right.
Because I am every Sunday morning in the sun:
the sound of the coffee pot when it runs out of water.
I've got a love so big she goes road tripping without me.
Because my chest is the size of a medicine cabinet
with the shelves pulled out,
and my heart always finds her way back,
even then.
If healing means I've got to set my heart free, a little while,
if it means I've got to let her see the world without me,
if it means she comes back big, and brave, and wizened,
while I live with my hands pressed to the empty place
where she used to be—
then so be it.
So be it, because it will be worth the day
she comes home,
and I open the hinge to my chest and remember
all the faces, all the love,
I've ever known.

POTTING SOIL

This is the boy you fell in love with
when you weren't supposed to.
The boy who kissed like the first day of spring.
The boy whose mother told him,
that so long as he ate enough sunflower seeds,
he could grow his own garden, on the inside.
He's got flowers in his stomach,
because he never knew
that he could swallow his heart
and grow love in his belly
like lilacs in June.
But, oh, sometimes—
sometimes, he makes himself so small
you think his ribs might bear down
and crush them.
And you can't repot a love like that,
it just wouldn't be suited to the soil.
There would never be room
for the roots to grow.
This boy has a stomach full of flowers,
and he never cries.
Has to save up all his water,
'cause it's the dry season in his chest
and he's got to make the most of
every last drop.
His flowers, they kept him delicate
when the elements tried
to make him harsh.
And on the bad days, he thinks back
to his mother's sunflower smile,
and how her garden had grown so big,
he swore he could see it blooming
just past her teeth.
He wants a garden like hers.
And you want a love made of sun
and soil.
He's got flowers in his stomach
and he's been learning, all his life,
to make them grow.

SWAMPLAND LOVE SONG

It was late summer,
with the stars peeking out
from a pebbled sky.
I sank into the mud
to the sound of frog song
and kissed the earth.
This is where I learned
that I am made of
swampland love songs:
a heart saturated to the root.
Where I learned my love isn't beautiful
the way open fields are beautiful.
I am like fallen trees in cluttered wetlands,
with feelings that sink beneath my skin—
I am changeable.
Slow-shifting.
I am mud at the waterside,
loving close to the ground.
Knowing me means getting your shoes dirty.
I grow cattails from my fingers,
I've got toadstools in my lungs.
But the trees are still growing,
just fine, here.
The trees are still growing,
just fine.

VENUS

She is the prayer I save to speak
until everyone else is sleeping:
the night sky cracked open like
the kind of sight madmen paint pictures of.
She stands at the stone steps of the universe—
the alpha and the omega:
Queen in every sense of the word that matters.
I am nothing but flesh, but she—
she holds the world on the tip of a spindle.
She kisses the hemispheres goodnight,
her lips painted the same colors you dream in.
I am in love with a cluster of stars,
spiraling out from the center of the universe.
Her hands, holy altars.
Her hands, asteroid belts.
Me: the singularity who swallowed a star,
to suck in as much of her light
as my hungry body could hold.
A woman like religion.
A woman everlasting.
A woman with eyes like deep space.

BEST FRIENDS WITH BENEFITS

I write to you like a lover
but we have never been in love.
Three AM and I'm sending snapshots
of my heart because you are the only one
who isn't afraid to look at them.
Sometimes we kiss for no reason.
Sometimes I go crawling into your bed
because I need a space to belong to
and your hands are steadier
than mine have ever been.
Sometimes you get lost
and you wind up on my doorstep,
but it's okay—
you know you're always welcome here.
I tell you the secrets I've been
keeping from myself while you
peel apart at the edges and admit
to all the soft things you pretend
you don't know how to feel.
We understand each other, here.
The frame of my bed knows all our demons.
We don't touch like that in the daytime,
but at night you are all hands
and I am all teeth
and we are a double-hinged door
slammed open by the wind.
We work that way.
It's easy as breathing:
two kindred souls wrapped up together,
shaking hands with the universe,
bound in the same skin.

I WANT TO TELL YOU YOU ARE BEAUTIFUL

You think you are an ocean,
with skin like salt water,
the knobs of your spine
barnacles
that get stuck to my mouth
when I kiss you.

You think you are so deep,
so vast,
I'll be lost in you.
As if I have never gone plunging
into the pit of my own heart.
As if I have never found
my way back out.

You think that letting me in
is like taking the last thing
that's keeping me floating.
Like I'll be stranded—
treading water—
until the sea swallows me whole.

As if you could swallow me whole.
As if you were made
for a feat like that.
You are not the ocean.
You are in it.
And you're not taking
the breath from me.
I'm trying to give you yours.

(I don't have to love you
to want your head to stay
above water.
I don't have to love you
to want you to make it out okay.)

TWENTY-FOUR

Two months in and all you know
is your new medication
makes your hands shake.
Twenty-four years old,
and you're finally starting to understand
that calling a place home
doesn't make it feel like one.
Yesterday, you changed your first tire,
but you still don't know how to love someone
without cracking your ribs open
and spilling through the fault lines
like some kind of natural disaster.
You pretend that if you keep laughing
you won't have to admit you're afraid;
pretending like love's gonna
solve all your problems;
pretending you've got it all together
when you don't have it together at all.
You have made so much
out of so little—
built yourself tall
on the backs of every person
who said that you couldn't.
You flew your colors in a war zone—
made it back wounded and alive.
You have done everything you know how to,
and it means something
to have tried.

BUT YOU LEAVE THEM

The girls who love you
keep slipping through your fingers
after all of this talk of how
certain you are that they
deserve better.
This is how you push women
out of your life with mouthfuls
of good intentions.
You know what you're doing.
But they were always
so beautiful and so kind
and you never believed
you could love them right.
Not when you loved like the
rusty joints of rattling train cars.
You've never had hands like
a midsummer sunset, but god—
you loved a woman who did.
She was too much for you.
Too real, too alive.
She kissed the crickets
from your lungs, and you
forgot how to speak in the face
of her fearless quiet.
Like handspun glory,
like the divots in a hardwood floor—
her skin was soft and dark and holy,
and you were lying
when you said
you didn't love her
anymore.

FLASHBANG

I set fire to the palms of my hands
two nights after the first time you kissed them.
Truth is, with you, I never got my sea legs.
We were stuttering through waltzes our
feet didn't know the words to
and I got caught up keeping time.
I still touch you like some sort of relic
that I'm half afraid of; all the while,
the holy of your hips rings so loud
that the rest of the world shrinks
to the echo of the ocean in a seashell.
Love is a word for idealists,
a word for romantics,
for people who have never tasted their name
on the crest of your lips:
crashing like a wave against my ribs.
You are not a tender four letter word.
You are words unwelcome in polite company:
words I am not supposed to say, but that slip, broken,
from my mouth when your hands
find my waist without warning.
Those kinds of four letter words.
You are the crash of cymbals—my own undoing.
And I am a wandering disciple in search of a doctrine
that can bring me to my knees.
You are the holy writ I caught fire to.
But I am the attic,
full of pictures you do not recognize—
lifetimes you do not think you've ever had.
My heart has always been caught
a few decades behind you
and you became the lifeline reeling me back
to the space inside of my ribs.
You are a far distant country,
and I am the late-night corner store
in the town where I grew up.
For all our wicked mythology,
I know you'll still forget me;
after all,
I have spent my whole life as a runner,
but you've already wandered
far enough.

WHY WE DIDN'T WORK OUT

I found my lipstick in the corner of your mouth
and chased it halfway down your spine.
You were always bad at waltzes
and my feet only knew two things:
how to keep time,
and how to walk away.
I didn't mean to spend so long counting.
But the bend in your spine
looked just like the valley
from my favorite painting,
by an artist whose name I can't remember.
And there, nestled against the curve of your skeleton:
that was where I wanted
to build a house
and make a home.
So if my heart dropped out of my mouth,
or my hands forgot themselves around you,
it was only because I was imagining the way
you would kiss my neck while I poured my coffee
or the way
I never wanted a picket fence kind of life
until I met you.
If I put distance between
my heart and your mouth,
it's only because my ribcage was busy putting down roots
along the dip of your spine.
If I seemed nervous, or worried, or cripplingly afraid—
I was.

SUN SICKNESS

I caught your name
like dust in sunlight:
syllables splayed on the pads of my fingers.
I closed my open palm to find you
missing.
The sunbeam of you speckled on my knuckles,
a laugh in the breeze
that escaped out the window
through the crack in the
foundation
of the bravado
I am built on.
I chased the wind to find a whisper
and everything I thought I knew
pulled apart, like cobwebs
on the breeze.
More legend than skin,
you are worked into the mythology of my heartbeats.
And I am more idle wanderer than reckless adventurer.
I go looking but I never seem to leave—
Hours spent haunting my own back yard
until I'm dried up from the sun,
sick down to my bones with wanting things
I was never brave enough to take
for my own.

OLD SOULS

It's you and I,
sightseeing around the oldest town in Texas,
with its brick buildings
that look like infants
next to the ancient atoms in our skin.
Holding hands through moss-covered alleyways,
we are older than the cracked foundations and sullied windowpanes.
There are words on our tongues that could make the Parthenon
feel young again.
We are old on the inside,
where the last wheeze of a dying star
still echoes through the universe,
masked by the sounds of our voice.

It's you and I.
I am in your mouth; I am curled up
next to your bones
and they hum my name the way
Gregorian monks sing of God.
I wonder if they've always known me—
if every cell in your body has just been waiting for me
to come home.
I tell them I am here now.
I let my bones sing with your bones.
We are the kind of harmonies
that make the moon rise, at night.
We are the reason the tide comes in.

It's you and I.
When they write of young lovers,
they are writing about the way
your body feels against mine, in the dark.
Your mouth loved me better than any god.
I was the altar you lay prostrate in front of;
you were the confessional where my sins
grew tongues
and learned to talk.

We are ancient, you and I.
We are clumsy newborns with curious hands.
We are the stars that caught fire in the cosmos
generations before the Earth pressed it's molten clay together.
Once—we were the youngest creatures to ever exist.
Now, we are poets and landmines.
We are volatile and reckless and in love.

DELICATE THINGS

Girl, you've got grit under your nails
that could bring a grown man to his knees.
That unforgiving powder keg in your chest
has been lighting up like midday in July
and you are not afraid of the fallout.
This is how you kept standing.
This is how you were strong enough,
to dig the fear out of your chest
and brave enough to let it back in.
With every dark thought you've ever had
in a row on your bedside table,
you kiss each one goodnight,
and again every morning.
Years back, you stopped trying to file down
the sharper sides of you.
Because you are not a history
with all the bad parts burned out—
you are a monument,
pulled up from the belly of the sea,
teeth like a leviathan.
You open your maw and let the water in.
And every wave that crashed against you,
every hand print left seared on your thighs,
you gave it a name and a goodbye,
and stretched up toward the sunlight.
If people could see the monsters
and the flowers
in the framework of you,
they would fall to their knees.
They would kiss your feet,
count your name as holy—love you like gospel.
You've been walking through fire
since they first put you on your feet,
and you are not afraid to blister
any more than you are afraid to cry.
And every mouth who has ever been scared to love you
never knew exactly why.

Ashe is a queer poet from Texas. She has nearly finished undergrad at Stephen F. Austin State University, where she majored in theatre and minored in gender studies. Ashe's focus falls, again and again, on themes of self-acceptance. She likes to give the demons room to breathe and she has always looked to the stars.

On top of poetry, Ashe is a playwright, an actor, and an artist.

Ashe hopes to move to a big city with her grumpy cat and cover herself in tattoos.

Other titles available from
WORDS DANCE PUBLISHING

I EAT CROW + BLUE COLLAR AT BEST
Poetry by Amanda Oaks + Zach Fishel

| $15 | 124 pages | 5.5" x 8.5" | softcover |

Home is where the heart is and both poets' hearts were raised in the Appalachian region of Western Pennsylvania surrounded by coal mines, sawmills, two-bit hotel taverns, farms, churches and cemeteries. These poems take that region by the throat and shake it until it's bloody and then, they breathe it back to life. This book is where you go when you're looking for nostalgia to kick you in the teeth. This is where you go when you're 200 miles away from a town you thought you'd never want to return to but suddenly you're pining for it.

Amanda and Zach grew up 30 miles from each other and met as adults through poetry. Explore both the male and female perspective of what it's like to grow up hemmed in by an area's economic struggle. These poems mine through life, love, longing and death, they're for home and away, and the inner strength that is not deterred by any of those things.

SPLIT BOOK #1

What are Split Books?

Two full-length books from two poets in one + there's a collaborative split between the poets in the middle!

COLLECT THEM ALL!

Other titles available from
WORDS DANCE PUBLISHING

SHAKING THE TREES
Poetry by Azra Tabassum

| $12 | 72 pages | 5.5" x 8.5" | softcover |

ISBN: 978-0692232408

From the very first page *Shaking the Trees* meets you at the edge of the forest, extends a limb & seduces you into taking a walk through the dark & light of connection. Suddenly, like a gunshot in the very-near distance, you find yourself traipsing though a full-blown love story that you can't find your way out of because the story is actually the landscape underneath your feet. It's okay though, you won't get lost– you won't go hungry. Azra shakes every tree along the way so their fruit blankets the ground before you. She picks up pieces & hands them to you but not before she shows you how she can love you so gently it will feel like she's unpeeling you carefully from yourself. She tells you that it isn't about the bite but the warm juice that slips from the lips down chin. She holds your hand when you're trudging through the messier parts, shoes getting stuck in the muck of it all, but you'll keep going with the pulp of the fruit still stuck in-between your teeth, the juice will dry in the crooks of your elbows & in the lines on your palms. You'll taste bittersweet for days.

"I honestly haven't read a collection like this before, or at least I can't remember having read one. My heart was wrecked by Azra. It's like that opening line in Fahrenheit 451 when Bradbury says, "It was a pleasure to burn." It really was a pleasure being wrecked by it."

— **NOURA**
of *NouraReads*

"I wanted to cry and cheer and fuck. I wanted to take the next person I saw and kiss them straight on the lips and say, "Remember this moment for the rest of your life."

— **CHELSEA MILLER**

Other titles available from
WORDS DANCE PUBLISHING

SPARKLEFAT

Poetry by Melissa May

| $12 | 62 pages | 5.5" x 8.5" | softcover |

SparkleFat is a loud, unapologetic, intentional book of poetry about my body, about your body, about fat bodies and how they move through the world in every bit of their flash and spark and burst. Some of the poems are painful, some are raucous celebrations, some are reminders and love letters and quiet gifts back to the vessel that has traveled me so gracefully - some are a hymnal of yes, but all of them sparkle. All of them don't mind if you look – really. They built their own house of intention, and they draped that shit in lime green sequins. All of them intend to be seen. All of them have no more fucks to give about a world that wants them to be quiet.

"I didn't know how much I needed this book until I found myself, three pages in, ugly crying on the plane next to a concerned looking business man. This book is the most glorious, glittery pink permission slip. It made me want to go on a scavenger hunt for every speck of shame in my body and sing hot, sweaty R&B songs to it. There is no voice more authentic, generous and resounding than Melissa May. From her writing, to her performance, to her role in the community she delivers fierce integrity & staggering passion. From the first time I watched her nervously step to the mic, to the last time I watched her crushed me in a slam, it is has been an honor to watch her astound the poetry slam world and inspire us all to be not just better writers but better people. We need her."

— **LAUREN ZUNIGA**
Author of *The Smell of Good Mud*

"*SparkleFat* is a firework display of un-shame. Melissa May's work celebrates all of the things we have been so long told deserved no streamers. This collection invites every fat body out to the dance and steams up the windows in the backseat of the car afterwards by kissing the spots we thought (or even hoped) no one noticed but are deserving of love just the same as our mouths."

— **RACHEL WILEY**
Author of the forthcoming *Fat Girl Finishing School*

Other titles available from
WORDS DANCE PUBLISHING

WHAT WE BURIED
Poetry by Caitlyn Siehl

| $12 | 64 pages | 5.5" x 8.5" | softcover |

ISBN: 978-0615985862

This book is a cemetery of truths buried alive. The light draws you in where you will find Caitlyn there digging. When you get close enough, she'll lean in & whisper, Baby, buried things will surface no matter what, get to them before they get to you first. Her unbounded love will propel you to pick up a shovel & help— even though the only thing you want to do is kiss her lips, kiss her hands, kiss every one of her stretch marks & the fire that is raging in pit of her stomach. She'll see your eyes made of devour & sadness, she'll hug you & say, Baby, if you eat me alive, I will cut my way out of your stomach. Don't let this be your funeral. Teach yourself to navigate the wound.

"It takes a true poet to write of love and desire in a way that manages to surprise and excite. Caitlyn Siehl does this in poem after poem and makes it seem effortless. Her work shines with a richness of language and basks in images that continue to delight and astound with multiple readings. What We Buried is a treasure from cover to cover."

— **WILLIAM TAYLOR JR.**
Author of *An Age of Monsters*

Other titles available from
WORDS DANCE PUBLISHING

LITERARY SEXTS

A Collection of Short & Sexy Love Poems
(Volume 1)

| $12 | 42 pages | 5.5" x 8.5" | softcover |

ISBN: 978-0615959726

Literary Sexts is a modern day anthology of short love poems with subtle erotic undertones edited by Amanda Oaks & Caitlyn Siehl. Hovering around 50 contributors & 124 poems, this book reads is like one long & very intense conversation between two lovers. It's absolutely breathtaking. These are poems that you would text to your lover. Poems that you would slip into a back pocket, suitcase, wallet or purse on the sly. Poems that you would write on slips of paper & stick under your crush's windshield wiper. Poems that you would write on a Post-it note & leave on the bathroom mirror.

HIT #1 ON AMAZON'S HOT NEW RELEASE LIST!

"It's like 100+ new ways to make a reader blush. The imagery is so subtle yet completely thrilling..." **NOW I NEED A COLD SHOWER!"**
– K. W.

"**I DEVOURED IT!** I physically wanted to eat these poems. I wanted to wear them on my skin like perfume..."
– A. G.

"I have consumed this in ways that have left my insides looking like strips of velvet fabric... **SO ORGASMIC!**"
– K. B.

"**A MAELSTROM OF EMOTIONS!** I only hope that there is a Volume 2, a Volume 3 and so on because I need more of this!"
– Daniel CZ

Other titles available from
WORDS DANCE PUBLISHING

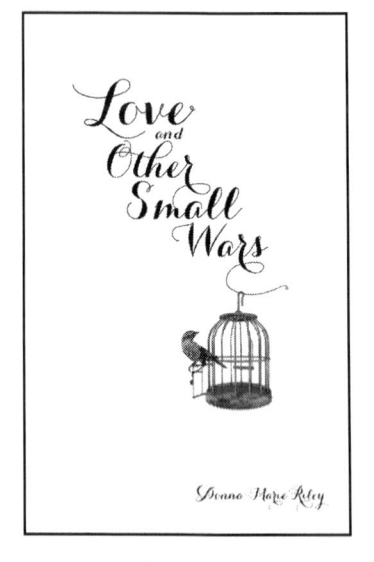

LOVE AND OTHER SMALL WARS

Poetry by Donna-Marie Riley

| $12 | 76 pages | 5.5" x 8.5" | softcover |

ISBN: 978-0615931111

Love and Other Small Wars reminds us that when you come back from combat usually the most fatal of wounds are not visible. Riley's debut collection is an arsenal of deeply personal poems that embody an intensity that is truly impressive yet their hands are tender. She enlists you. She gives you camouflage & a pair of boots so you can stay the course through the minefield of her heart. You will track the lovely flow of her soft yet fierce voice through a jungle of powerful imagery on womanhood, relationships, family, grief, sexuality & love, amidst other matters. Battles with the heart aren't easily won but Riley hits every mark. You'll be relieved that you're on the same side. Much like war, you'll come back from this book changed.

"Riley's work is wise, intense, affecting, and uniquely crafted. This collection illuminates her ability to write with both a gentle hand and a bold spirit. She inspires her readers and creates an indelible need inside of them to consume more of her exceptional poetry. I could read *Love and Other Small Wars* all day long…and I did."

— **APRIL MICHELLE BRATTEN**
editor of *Up the Staircase Quarterly*

"Riley's poems are personal, lyrical and so vibrant they practically leap off the page, which also makes them terrifying at times. A beautiful debut."

— **BIANCA STEWART**

Other titles available from
WORDS DANCE PUBLISHING

Tammy Foster Brewer is the type of poet who makes me wish I could write poetry instead of novels. From motherhood to love to work, Tammy's poems highlight the extraordinary in the ordinary and leave the reader wondering how he did not notice what was underneath all along. I first heard Tammy read 'The Problem is with Semantics' months ago, and it's stayed with me ever since. Now that I've read the entire collection, I only hope I can make room to keep every one of her poems in my heart and mind tomorrow and beyond.

— NICOLE ROSS, author

NO GLASS ALLOWED
Poetry by Tammy Foster Brewer

$12 | 56 pages | 6" x 9" | softcover | ISBN: 978-0615870007

Brewer's collection is filled with uncanny details that readers will wear like the accessories of womanhood. Fishing the Chattahoochee, sideways trees, pollen on a car, white dresses and breast milk, and so much more -- all parts of a deeply intellectual pondering of what is often painful and human regarding the other halves of mothers and daughters, husbands and wives, lovers and lost lovers, children and parents.

— NICHOLAS BELARDES
author of *Songs of the Glue Machines*

Tammy deftly juxtaposes distinct imagery with stories that seem to collide in her brilliant poetic mind. Stories of transmissions and trees and the words we utter, or don't. Of floods and forgiveness, conversations and car lanes, bread and beginnings, awe and expectations, desire and leaps of faith that leave one breathless, and renewed.

"When I say I am a poet / I mean my house has many windows" has to be one of the best descriptions of what it's like to be a contemporary female poet who not only holds down a day job and raises a family, but whose mind and heart regularly file away fleeting images and ideas that might later be woven into something permanent, and perhaps even beautiful. This ability is not easily acquired. It takes effort, and time, and the type of determination only some writers, like Tammy, possess and are willing to actively exercise.

— KAREN DEGROOT CARTER
author of *One Sister's Song*

Other titles available from
WORDS DANCE PUBLISHING

Unrequited love? We've all been there.

Enter:

WHAT TO DO AFTER SHE SAYS NO
by Kris Ryan.

This skillfully designed 10-part poem explores what it's like to ache for someone. This is the book you buy yourself or a friend when you are going through a breakup or a one-sided crush, it's the perfect balance between aha, humor & heartbreak.

WHAT TO DO AFTER SHE SAYS NO
A Poem by Kris Ryan

$10 | 104 pages | 5" x 8" | softcover | ISBN: 978-0615870045

"*What to Do After She Says No* takes us from Shanghai to the interior of a refrigerator, but mostly dwells inside the injured human heart, exploring the aftermath of emotional betrayal. This poem is a compact blast of brutality, with such instructions as "Climb onto the roof and jump off. If you break your leg, you are awake. If you land without injury, pinch and twist at your arm until you wake up." Ryan's use of the imperative often leads us to a reality where pain is the only outcome, but this piece is not without tenderness, and certainly not without play, with sounds and images ricocheting off each other throughout. Anticipate the poetry you wish you knew about during your last bad breakup; this poem offers a first "foothold to climb out" from that universal experience."

— **LISA MANGINI**

"Reading Kris Ryan's *What To Do After She Says No* is like watching your heart pound outside of your chest. Both an unsettling visual experience and a hurricane of sadness and rebirth—this book demands more than just your attention, it takes a little bit of your soul, and in the end, makes everything feel whole again."

— **JOHN DORSEY**
author of *Tombstone Factory*

"*What to Do After She Says No* is exquisite. Truly, perfectly exquisite. It pulls you in on a familiar and wild ride of a heart blown open and a mind twisting in an effort to figure it all out. It's raw and vibrant...and in the same breath comforting. I want to crawl inside this book and live in a world where heartache is expressed so magnificently."

— **JO ANNA ROTHMAN**
MA, Coach & Conjurer of Electric Creative Wholeness

WORDS DANCE PUBLISHING has one aim:

    To spread mind-blowing / heart-opening poetry.

Words Dance artfully & carefully wrangles words that were born to dance wildly in the heart-mind matrix. Rich, edgy, raw, emotionally-charged energy balled up & waiting to whip your eyes wild; we rally together words that were written to make your heart go boom right before they slay your mind. We like Poems that sneak up on you. Poems that make out with you. Poems that bloody your mouth just to kiss it clean. Poems that bite your cheek so you spend all day tonguing the wound. Poems that vandalize your heart. Poems that act like a tin can phone connecting you to your childhood. Fire Alarm Poems. Glitterbomb Poems. Jailbreak Poems. Poems that could marry the land or the sea; that are both the hero & the villain. Poems that are the matches when there is a city-wide power outage. Poems that throw you overboard just dive in & save your ass. Poems that push you down on the stoop in front of history's door screaming at you to knock. Poems that are soft enough to fall asleep on. Poems that will still be clinging to the walls inside of your bones on your 90th birthday. We like poems. Submit yours.

Words Dance Publishing is an independent press out of Pennsylvania. We work closely & collaboratively with all of our writers to ensure that their words continue to breathe in a sound & stunning home. Most importantly though, we leave the windows in these homes unlocked so you, the reader, can crawl in & throw one fuck of a house party.

To learn more about our books, authors, events & Words Dance Poetry Magazine, visit:

WORDSDANCE.COM

Printed in Great Britain
by Amazon